INSPECTING SPECIAL NEEDS PROVISION IN SCHOOLS

A PRACTICAL GUIDE

MARIA LANDY
AND CHARLES GAINS

David Fulton Publishers
London

David Fulton Publishers Ltd
2 Barbon Close London WC1N 3JX

First published in Great Britain by
David Fulton Publishers 1996

Note: The right of the authors to be identified as the authors of this work has been asserted by them in accordance with the Copyright Designs and Patents Act 1988.

Copyright © Maria Landy and Charles Gains

British Library Cataloguing in Publication in Data

A catalogue record for this book is available from the British Library

ISBN 1-85346-400-7

All rights reserved. No part of this publication may be reproduced, stored in a retrieval system or transmitted, in any form or by any means, electronic, mechanical, photocopying, recording or otherwise without the prior permission of the publishers.

Acknowledgement
In this book Crown Copyright is reproduced with the permission of the Controller of HMSO. Extracts have been used from the OFSTED Handbook Guidance on the Inspection of Special Schools pages 8, 9, & 10 Code of Practice on the Identification and Assessment of Special Needs and the Education Act 1992.

Typeset by The Harrington Consultancy Ltd. London
Printed in Great Britain by Bell and Bain Ltd Glasgow

Contents

The aim of this publication iv

The framework for inspections 1
Background of OFSTED inspections
Framework for the inspection of schools 1996
The inspection team
School inspection: Realities and opportunities
Pupil responses: Key questions on the quality of learning
Quality of teaching: Key questions
Use of time: Key questions

Pre-inspection considerations 9
Pre-inspection procedures
Advice for headteachers
Preparation for inspection
Preparation countdown
Documentation
Consultation
Self review

Inspecting special needs 17
What is a 'special educational need'?
A statement of entitlement
Code of Practice: Main features
The school's SEN policy statement
What is special?
SEN: Everyone's responsibility
Responsibilities of the Governing Body
SEN questions for senior management
SEN documentation
Documentation: A further check list
SEN implementation
SEN policy and practice: Key questions
Statements and annual reviews
Extending the experiences of SEN pupils
SEN focus during the inspection
Lesson observation
Special units in mainstream schools
Special schools
SEN and the school development plan
SEN: further evaluation questions
The special educational needs co-ordinator
The dynamic role of the SENCO
Interviewing co-ordinators

Post inspection 41
The report
The action plan
After the inspection

References 45

Appendices 47
A. Pupil responses: Attainment, attitudes and progress
B. Quality of teaching: Key points
C. Summary of the Inspection Report

The aim of this publication

The aim of this publication is to enable all those concerned with the education of pupils with special educational needs to:

- *understand* the legal framework and purpose of OFSTED inspection of schools
- *understand* how to prepare themselves properly for the process of inspection
- *understand* how to maximise the experience for the benefit of the pupils

The publication will be of interest to:

- Governors of schools and in particular those governors with responsibility for special educational needs
- The senior management team
- School working groups
- The special educational needs co-ordinator (SENCO)
- Teachers and support staff with responsibility for pupils with learning, sensory and physical difficulties.
- Concerned parents/carers and parent governors
- Those involved in training teachers and preparing schools for inspection

The format is designed to:

- act as an *aide-memoire* to those anticipating, or currently involved in, an inspection
- to be part of a training pack. Each page is complete and self-contained and can be photocopied for training purposes.

The publication is not designed to replace the *Framework for the Inspection of Schools*, the *Handbook for the Inspection of Schools* and other OFSTED publications. It should only be used in conjunction with these core texts.

The Framework for Inspections

Background of OFSTED Inspections

1989 Her Majesty's Inspectorate (HMI) celebrated 150 years of existence. At the time there were about 480 inspectors involved in all phases of education, including further and higher education, and teacher training.

1992 The Education (Schools) Act introduced a new system of school inspection.

The Office for Standards in Education (OFSTED) was created as a new non-ministerial department headed by a new Crown Office holder, Her Majesty's Chief Inspector of Schools (HMCI).

HMCI's main duty is to keep the Secretary of State informed about:

'... standards of achievement, quality of education, efficiency of management and the development of values in schools in England and Wales'.

1995 Following the earlier Framework for the Inspection of Schools (OFSTED, 1993) the revised Framework for the Inspection of Schools is published to take effect from April, 1996.

OFSTED ...

- ... has set up the new system for inspecting schools and is also responsible for the training of registered inspectors and team inspectors
- ... plans to inspect all schools every four years using mainly independent teams of inspectors. Inspections of secondary schools began in September 1993 and primary and special schools in September 1994
- ... arranges contracts for inspecting individual schools
- ... will operate as a professional network providing judgements and advice on aspects of educational provision
- ... will advise local authorities on issues and concerns arising from inspections.
- ... will advise the Secretary of State, Department for Education and Employment (DfEE) and other national bodies on the standards and quality of education

HMI

- ... will monitor the quality of OFSTED inspections and reports
- ... will undertake some inspections

Framework for the Inspection of Schools 1996

The 1996 framework aims to:

- ... make the inspection process more manageable for schools and inspectors
- ... sharpen judgements on the key issues of the quality of teaching and pupil achievement
- ... ensure that inspectors pay greater attention to a school's own evaluation of its strengths, weaknesses and priorities
- ... rid reports of jargon and make them more understandable to parents

The purpose of inspection

The purpose of inspection is to identify strengths and weaknesses so that schools may improve the quality of education they provide and raise the educational standards achieved by pupils. The published report and summary report provide information for parents and the local
community about the quality and standards of the school, consistent with the requirements of the Parents Charter. The inspection process, feedback and reports give direction to the school's strategy for planning, review and improvement by providing rigorous external evaluation and identifying key issues for action.

OFSTED (1995) *Framework for the Inspection of Schools* p5

Basis for inspection

The Education (Schools) Act 1992 requires inspectors to report on:

- the quality of the education provided by the school
- the educational standards achieved in the school
- whether the financial resources made available to the school are managed efficiently
- the spiritual, moral, social and cultural development of pupils at the school

Framework for the Inspection of Schools p5

Study the Inspection Schedule in the *Framework for the Inspection of Schools* pp12–15

The Inspection Team

The inspection team

- A Registered Inspector (RI) leads the team
- The Registered Inspector puts together a team of trained inspectors capable of inspecting all aspects of the school and each area of the National Curriculum
- The team must also include one or more inspectors charged with inspecting or co-ordinating the inspection of:

  –equal opportunities
  –special educational needs (where relevant)
  –the education of pupils for whom English is an additional language (where relevant)

- Every team will include a 'lay inspector' who has to be someone without personal experience of managing or working in a school

Standard and quality of inspection

The Registered Inspector must ensure that the team judgements are:

- secure, in that they are rooted in a substantial evidence base and informed by specified quantitative indicators
- first-hand, in that they are based largely on direct observation of pupils' work and teachers' work
- reliable, in that they are based on consistent application of the evaluation criteria in the inspection schedule contained within the Framework
- valid, in that they reflect what is actually achieved and provided by the school
- comprehensive, in that they cover all aspects of the school set out in the inspection schedule and in the contract specification
- corporate, in that the conclusions about the school as a whole reflect the collective view of the inspection team

Code of conduct for inspectors

Inspectors should:

- carry out their work with professionalism, integrity and courtesy
- evaluate the work of the school objectively
- report honestly and fairly
- communicate clearly and frankly
- act in the best interests of the pupils at the school
- respect the confidentiality of personal information

Taken from *Framework for the Inspection of Schools* pp6–7

School Inspection: Realities and Opportunities

- Inspection will be highly structured, costed and undertaken under a strict timetable

- The inspection team _is_ experienced and at least one member will have knowledge of, and responsibility for, special educational needs

- The main focus is on classroom observation which includes pupils with special educational needs

- The inspection is based on a thorough and a fair collection of evidence

- Inspections are judgmental, not negotiable and evidence based, using specified criteria

- Evidence for the inspection report is based on sampling from identified issues

- There is limited feedback time which must be carefully managed and arranged

- It is important that the headteacher works closely with the Registered Inspector. If the staff have any difficulties they should inform the headteacher who can relay them to the Registered Inspector

Pupil responses: Key Questions on the Quality of Learning

In assessing the quality of learning and the pupil responses, particularly attainment, attitudes and progress the inspection team will address some key questions. These include:

- What is the quality of learning taking place in this school?
- Is the learning at an appropriate pace?
- Are pupils gaining in knowledge, understanding and skills?
- What is their ability in reading, writing, numeracy and oracy?
- Does the pupils' attainment meet or exceed that expected for their ages?
- Are opportunities provided for observation and information seeking?
- Are pupils given the chance to look for patterns and deeper understanding?
- Are they encouraged to pose questions and solve problems?
- Can they apply their knowledge in unfamiliar situations?
- Are they involved in evaluating their own work and do they reflect on it and link it with past experience?
- Do they demonstrate the ability to concentrate and partake in sustained activities?
- Do they co-operate with each other?
- Are they sufficiently motivated?
- Do they respond to the challenges set by teachers with confidence, appropriate attitudes and adaptability?
- Are the pupils making progress and how can this be demonstrated? e.g.
  – Records of achievement
  – Past records and reports to parents
  – Named, dated examples of work over time
  – Video evidence of progress
  – Schools' self analysis and review procedures
  – Targets achieved in IEPs
  – Annual review reports
  – Parents' and pupils' comments and perceptions

See Appendix A for a checklist on pupil's attainment, attitudes and progress

> **The inspection team will be better informed if the school is well prepared. Should there be aspects of the school that generate justifiable pride these should be conveyed to the team.**

Quality of Teaching: Key Questions

In a similar way to assessing the quality of learning inspectors will comment on the quality of teaching. Key questions here will include:

- Were appropriate goals set for whole classes, groups and individuals?
- Were the activities planned and well presented?
- Is the content appropriate and motivating?
- Was the organisation and management effective?
- Was a range of teaching skills in evidence?
- Was the pace appropriate?
- Could progression and rigour be demonstrated?
- Was there feedback to the students?
- How was the work monitored or evaluated?
- What was the quality of any support assistants or teachers?
- Were the pupil groupings suitable?
- Was the subject well covered with a clear command and secure knowledge base?
- Was there evidence of differentiation and planning to meet individual needs?
- Were resources well planned, organised and used?
- Were the expectations and standards achieved appropriate?

See Appendix B for further notes on quality of teaching

Prior to an inspection it is a useful exercise to work through an appropriate checklist with one teacher, perhaps, evaluating the quality of learning in a colleague's lessons and vice-versa.

Use of Time: Key Questions

The inspection team will ask questions related to the effective use of time. These will include:

- Is there sufficient and appropriate time allocated to different subjects at each key stage?
- Are all pupils receiving a broad and balanced curriculum?
- Is there a marked variation between classes?
- Do lessons start and finish on time?
- Does the school use a common format and language to allocate time and how is the timetable monitored?

The taught hours per week will be inspected.

Schools should carefully calculate actual teaching times and ascertain whether they are in line with DfEE recommendations. These are:

Key Stage	DfEE recommended
1	21.00
2	23.50
3	24.00
4	25.00

Wide variations were found in allocated time in many inspections during 1992–94

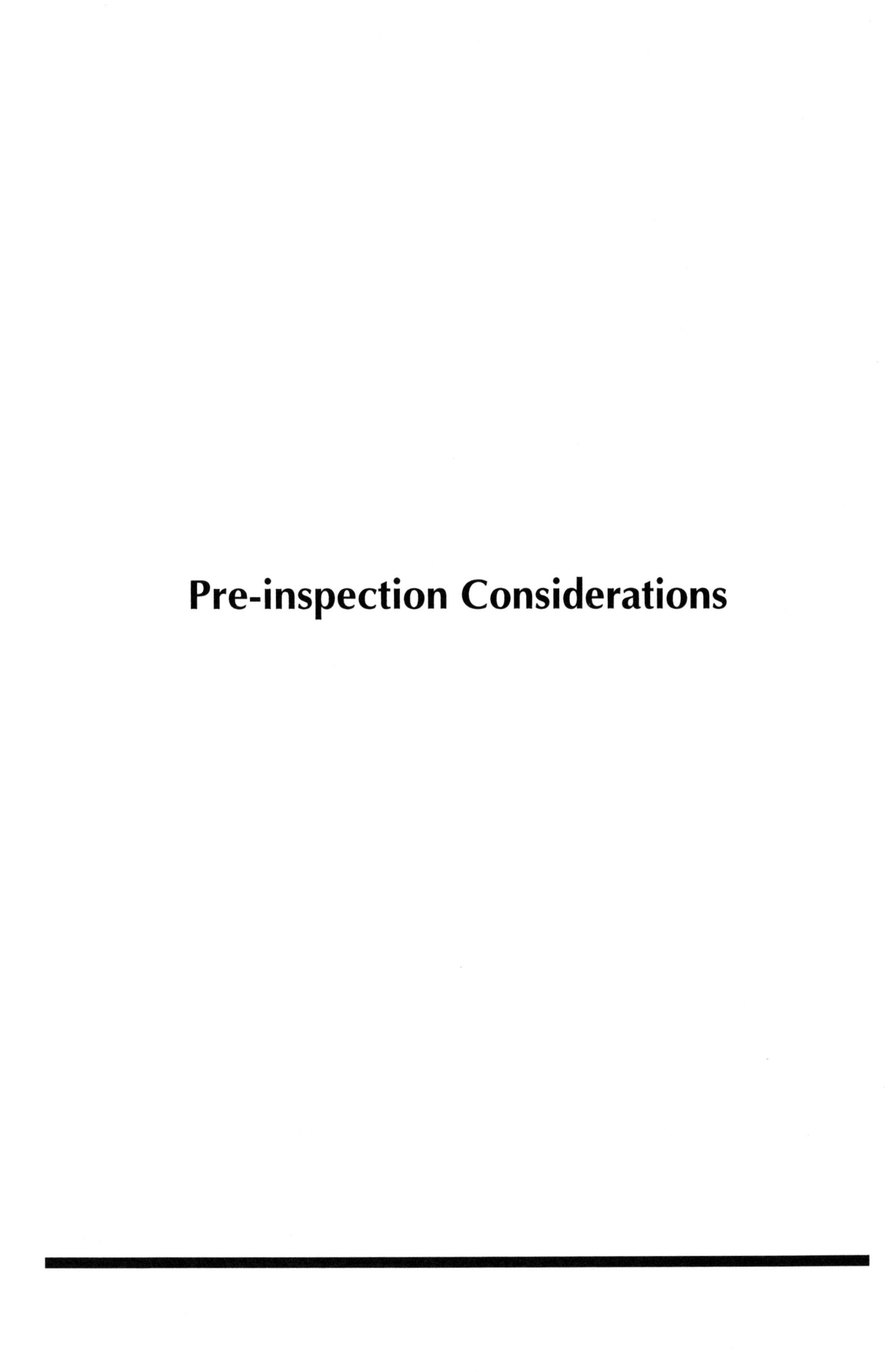

Pre-inspection Considerations

Pre-inspection Procedures

OFSTED will:

- inform the school when it is due for inspection
- agree with the Governing Body a specification which will be put out to tender by OFSTED
- look for at least two tenders
- award the contract to a chosen Registered Inspector

The Governing Body will:

- arrange for the Registered Inspector to meet parents at a mutually convenient time
- give parents at least three weeks notice of the meeting and enclose a statement or letter from the Registered Inspector
- invite parents to fill out a questionnaire to be returned to the Registered Inspector

The Headteacher must provide the inspection team with:

- relevant documentation
- access to lessons and other school activities
- opportunities to consult with pupils, staff, governors and other concerned individuals

---

The school is normally given at least a term's notice.

Advice for Headteachers

When the letter arrives don't panic! There is ample time to prepare.

Study the *Handbook for the Inspection of Schools* thoroughly so you fully understand what the inspection team is looking for.

Pass on to staff relevant sections of the Handbook for their consideration.

Arrange meetings and training for staff.

List the school's strengths and weaknesses.

Ensure your school policy statements and other documentation is up to date and in order.

Identify discrepancies between published statements and practice.

Draw up a timetable of events.

Budget for increased paperwork!

Keep governors fully aware of developments.

Consider what you want the school to get out of the inspection.

Preparation for Inspection

- Study *Framework for the Inspection of Schools* and have it available at all times
- Ensure that the school completes the initial form from OFSTED *fully*
- Prepare all relevant documentation about various aspects of the school and present them in a *coherent* package
- All documentation is required in *advance*
- Generally the inspection will last *approximately* a week
- There is a *minimum* number of inspection days to be spent in the school as set out in the contract
- The number of inspection days *varies* according to the *size* and *type* of school
- It is important that schools seek specific pre-inspection *advice* particularly from the local authority
- *Briefings* should take place at various levels – governors, senior management, staff etc
- Briefing *topics* might include:
    - Finance
    - Health and Safety
    - The school development plan
    - Co-ordinator's roles and responsibilities
    - The inspection week
    etc

The role of Senior Managers is to:

- prepare the staff and governors
- provide the Registered Inspector with documentation and optional additional information
- plan the week, arrange timetables, interviews and discussion opportunities

---

Remember that the inspection team is required to demonstrate that their judgements are secure, first hand, reliable, valid, comprehensive and corporate

Preparation Countdown

1. Consult local authority or other forms of support for advice
2. Brief governors
3. Brief staff
4. Senior Management Team to study the *Handbook*
5. Staff to study relevant sections of the *Handbook*
6. Documentation audit
7. Briefing of non-teaching staff
8. Accelerate classroom observations and school self review
9. Inform parents
10. Discuss with pupils
11. Registered Inspector visits
12. Parents meeting and questionnaires
13. Clarify plans for inspection week
14. Lesson proformas prepared
15. The inspection week
16. Post-inspection feedback
17. Prepare the press release
18. Prepare the Action Plan
19. Copy of report summary/action plan distributed
20. Revise the school development plan

Documentation

Information required by the inspectors:

- Details of the school population and catchment areas
- National Curriculum assessment (and examination results where applicable)
- Attendance and exclusion data
- Budget information
- How the curriculum and teaching groups are organised
- Staff composition, qualifications and employment
- Details of accommodation and resources

Additional documentation will include:

1. The School Development Plan
2. Current prospectus including the aims and objectives of the school
3. The staff handbook
4. Financial auditor's report
5. Attainment on admission
6. Support for pupils with special educational needs
7. Recent annual report to governors by the headteacher
8. Recent annual report by governors to parents
9. Governor's policy statements
10. School policy statements
11. Schemes of work
12. Curriculum guidelines
13. School/class timetables
14. Staff development policy
15. Job descriptions
16. Staff meeting programme
17. Extra curricular activities
18. School's external links
19. Special educational needs register
20. Details regarding accreditation, records of achievement, links and destinations *etc*

Additionally the school may wish to present photographic and video evidence of major events, festivals, visits, residential experiences, productions etc

---

Consultation

Consultation

The inspection team will want to have discussions with:

- Governors
- Parents
- Pupils
- Educational psychologists
- Educational Welfare Officers
- Other agencies
- Headteacher
- Senior management
- Heads of Department
- Year Tutors
- Special educational needs co-ordinator
- Support staff

Parents

Schedule 2 of the *1992 Education Act* requires the appropriate authority of the school to arrange a meeting of the Registered Inspector and those parents of pupils at the school who wish to attend. The appropriate authority of a school without a delegated budget is the local education authority (LEA) and for an independent school it is the Proprietor. In all other cases it is the Governing body. The Registered Inspector should ensure that parents' views are sought on the aspects of the school specified in the *Inspection Schedule*. Their views will provide valuable background information and must be taken into account in the course of the inspection. As the regulations stipulate that the meeting is to take place before the inspection it will not be possible for the Registered Inspector to respond at this stage to parents' views of the school.

The Registered Inspector will, as soon after the meeting as possible, share the findings of the meeting with the Headteacher and Chairperson of the Governing Body. Where inspection reports refer to views expressed by parents they should indicate the extent to which inspection findings support those views. A questionnaire is also circulated to parents by the Headteacher and returned to the Registered Inspector. A summary of this is given to the school by the Registered Inspector.

Parents who help within the school may be interviewed as part of the inspection week and if they are involved in extra-curricular activities or use the facilities of the school this too may form part of the inspection. Parents' views are sought on the educational standards achieved, the quality of education provided, the pupils' spiritual, moral, social and cultural development and the management and efficiency of the school.

Pupils

It is important that pupils are informed as to the nature of the inspection as they will be observed, asked questions, be heard read and their work analysed.

Self Review

Subject audit
Headteacher and staff should:
- Read the *Inspection Handbook* and accompanying documentation
- Identify key issues for review
- Review by discussion with colleagues and classroom observation
- Use the results of this audit to inform the *School Development Plan*

Aspect audit
Governors, headteacher and staff should:
- Create a list from the *Handbook*
- Identify those aspects you plan to review
- Allocate responsibilities
- Link the outcomes with the School Development Plan

Efficiency
Governors, headteachers and relevant staff should:
- Read *Keeping Your Balance*
- Consider the checklists and recommendations
- Identify areas for review and development
- Allocate responsibilities
- Link the outcomes to the *School Development Plan*

Health and safety
Governors, headteacher and staff should:
- Provide all staff with guidance about health and safety
- Identify changes in policy or practice that are needed
- Implement those changes
- Monitor and evaluate the changes
- Link the outcomes to the *School Development Plan*

Inspecting Special Educational Needs

What is a 'Special Educational Need'?

There has always been confusion about defining special educational needs. Terminology has constantly changed over the years. There are two broad distinctions ie between legal and working definitions.

The legal position

The 1992 Education Act states, somewhat ambiguously, that:

'... a child has 'special needs' if he (*sic*) has a learning difficulty which calls for special educational provision to be made for him'.

Further . . .
'... child has a 'learning difficulty' if he:
(a)   has a significant greater difficulty in learning than the majority of children of his age
(b)   has a disability which either prevents or hinders him from making use of the educational facilities of a kind generally provided for children of his age in schools within the area of the local authority, *or*
(c)   is under the age of five years and is, or would be if special educational provision were made for him, likely to fall within paragraph (a) or (b) when over that age'

'special educational provision means ...
(a)   in relation to a child who has attained the age of two years, educational provision which is additional to, or otherwise different from, the educational provision made generally for children of his age in schools maintained by the local education authority or grant maintained schools in their area, and
(b)   in relation to a child under that age, educational provision of any kind'

Working definition

Clearly some pupils have difficulties which constrain them from maximum access to the curriculum and extra-curricular activities of the school, compared to their contemporaries. These constraints may be one or a combination of the following:

physical, intellectual, emotional, social, sensory or lack of educational opportunity

This special educational need may be: temporary or mild, intermediate or moderate, long term or severe.

The purpose of this explanation is to try to avoid labels or categorisations which bedevil the area and to indicate that most human beings, at some point, might experience a difficulty which impedes their learning. If this concept is used and accepted special educational needs become part of, and are integral, to the general education of all pupils.

> **We should look for an explanation and philosophy that encourages whole school responsibility and not promote the marginalisation of some pupils**

A Statement of Entitlement

The National Association for Special Educational Needs (NASEN) principles, aims and objectives are encapsulated in the following statement of entitlement:

- **E**ntitlement to a broad, balanced, relevant and differentiated education is a right for all.
- **N**either gender, race, creed nor exceptional needs should constrain individual entitlement.
- **T**rained and qualified personnel are essential for the delivery of quality education.
- **I**ndividual learners should be involved in decisions about their educational programme and provision.
- **T**houghtful assessment and testing should be used to the benefit of the learner.
- **L**earning is most effective when it takes place in a happy, sensitive and secure environment.
- **E**quality of opportunity must be integral to the planning of educational provision.
- **M**aximum participation by parents and carers must be secured in order to achieve partnership in education.
- **E**ducators should utilize teaching strategies which are responsive to different learning styles, and which ensure effective learning.
- **N**otable achievements by all learners should be recognised and recorded.
- **T**otal commitment to the principles of educational entitlement must be the responsibility of everyone in an inclusive society.

© The National Association for Special Educational Needs (NASEN)

Code of Practice: Main Features

- All schools must have a detailed SEN policy
- All schools must appoint a special educational needs co-ordinator (SENCO) to administer procedures
- There is a five stage assessment and provision procedure:
  - Stage 1 Class based
  - 2 Class based plus SENCO
  - 3 School plus external expertise
  - 4 Statutory assessment
  - 5 Statement
- Detailed process of assessment, recording and review at each stage
- Schools usually have responsibility to make and record provision at stages 1–3
- Nature of the provision by schools is to be specified
- Many pupils with SEN are to have Individual Education Plans (IEPs)
- Statementing and annual review procedures are strengthened
- Parental involvement throughout the process is required
- Local authority to monitor stage 3 and annual reviews closely

---

The Code of Practice is the most important document relating to special educational needs. It should be studied by senior management, the governors with responsibility for special educational needs and, in particular, the SENCO. An inspection team will expect a school to be fully aware of its contents and to have taken cognisance of its recommendations.

The School's SEN Policy Statement

(Code of Practice on the Identification and Assessment of Special Educational Needs, 1994, DFE, pp8–9)

As part of their statutory duties governing bodies of all maintained schools must publish information about, and report on, the school's policy on special educational needs. The information they must provide is:

1. Basic information about the school's special educational provision:
- the objectives of the school's SEN policy
- the name of the school's SEN co-ordinator or teacher responsible for the day-to-day operation of the SEN policy
- the arrangements for co-ordinating educational provision for pupils with SEN
- admission arrangements
- any SEN specialism and any special units
- any special facilities which increase or assist access to the school by pupils with SEN

2. Information about the school's policies for identification, assessment and provision for all pupils with special needs:
- the allocation of resources to and amongst pupils with SEN
- identification and assessment arrangements; and review procedures
- arrangements for providing access for pupils to a balanced and broadly based curriculum, including the National Curriculum
- how children with special needs are integrated within the school as a whole
- criteria for evaluating the success of a school's SEN policy
- arrangements for considering complaints about special educational provision within the school

3. Information about the school's staffing policies and partnership with bodies beyond the schools:
- the school's arrangements for in-service training
- use made of teachers and facilities from outside the school, including support services
- arrangements for partnership with parents
- links with other mainstream schools and special schools, including arrangements when pupils change or leave school
- links with health and social services, educational welfare services and any voluntary organisations

Educational (Special Educational Needs) (Information) Regulations, regulation 2 and Schedule 1

The annual report for each school shall include a report containing such information as may be prescribed about the implementation of the governing body's policy for pupils with special educational needs.
Section 161(5)

Inspectors will check that the school's SEN policy is accurate, up to date and being implemented
---

What is Special?

All schools are inspected in relation to their aims and purpose. It is vital that these are clearly stated and understood. While these have general applicability they also need to be viewed from the point of pupils with special educational needs. For example:

Our school's purpose is:

- to maximise individual potential
- to value the individual
- to promote self awareness and respect for others
- to provide a supportive caring environment
- to celebrate success in all its forms
- to create an ethos of high expectation
- to create a stimulating learning environment
  etc

Inspectors will have to assess if these aims are being met in respect of *all* pupils but will be particularly concerned that no pupil, irrespective of a disability or learning difficulty, is excluded in any way from the general purposes of the school

> **Specifically the inspection team will want to establish that special educational needs is the concern of every staff member, not just that of a designated person**

SEN: Everyone's Responsibility

It is important to consider special educational needs as integral to the design of all schemes of work and programmes of study.

Some questions for all teachers and support staff.

- Will the purpose of the activities and the means of achieving them be understood and welcomed by all pupils?
- Are the aims and objectives clear?
- Are the activities matched to pupils' differing:
    paces ... styles of learning ... abilities ... previous experience?
- Is time and order of priority allocated accordingly?
- Are tasks and activities chosen and presented to enable pupils with a wide range of abilities to experience success?
- Is there emphasis on oral work, at times, rather than written work to help pupils with learning difficulties?
- Is there a range of communication methods used for pupils with language difficulties?
- Are the activities broken down into a series of small and achievable steps for pupils who have marked learning difficulties?
- Will the activities stretch pupils of whom too little may have been expected in the past?
- Are there cross-curricular themes running through the work?
- How will teaching and, where available, support staff be deployed?
- Are there clear procedures for assessing, recording, reviewing and evaluating pupils' progress?
- How well is achievement reported?

It is recognised that failure to learn may result from teaching arrangements made or from inappropriate curriculum materials as well as a pupil's own difficulties.

Responsibilities of the Governing Body

School governing bodies have important statutory responsibilities towards pupils with special educational needs. The governing body must:

- do their best to ensure that the necessary provision is made for any pupil who has special educational needs
- ensure that, where the headteacher or the appropriate governor has been informed by the local educational authority that a pupil has special educational needs, those needs are made known to all who are likely to teach him or her
- ensure that teachers in the school are aware of the importance of identifying, and providing for, those pupils who have special educational needs
- draw up and report annually to parents on their policy for pupils with special educational needs
- ensure that the pupil joins in the activities of the school together with pupils who do not have special educational needs, so far as this is reasonably practical and compatible with the pupil receiving the necessary special educational provision, the efficient education of other children and the efficient use of resources

Education Act 1992, Section 161

Governors have huge responsibilities in relation to special educational needs and are a very important element in school inspection

SEN Questions for Senior Management

Senior management need to address the following questions. Does our school ensure that:

- a member of the Senior Management Team (SMT) has direct responsibility for special educational needs?
- there is a clearly designated member of staff (SENCO) responsible for co-ordinating schoolwide provision for special educational needs?
- governors are fully informed about special needs provision?
- the governors with SEN responsibility are in close contact with the SENCO?
- access to the National Curriculum for pupils with special needs is monitored and evaluated?
- the school policy for SEN is operational and effective?
- all staff have knowledge of pupils with SEN and are aware of their responsibilities in this area?
- there are school-wide procedures on recording, reviewing and evaluating pupils' progress?
- there are adequate resources, support and training for staff in dealing with pupils with special educational needs?
- transition procedures and post-school placements are clear?
- management of pupil behaviour is consistent throughout the school?
- there are regular evaluations of the effectiveness of school provision?

Are school policies and procedures understood by all participants and are they fully co-ordinated

SEN Documentation

The school should submit to the Registered Inspector documents that:

- *contain* the whole school special needs policy and *how* it will be put into practice
- *describe* the provision made for pupils with special educational needs including special provision for statemented pupils
- *list* the children with statements and accompanying details
- *give* samples of statements plus accompanying documentation
- *list* the non-statemented pupils deemed to have special needs and accompanying details
- *include* examples of Individual Education Plans/Programmes
- *detail* any special timetable arrangements
- *give* precise details of any support given to individuals, groups or classes
- *determine* whether able learners are included in provision
- *state* the arrangements for identification and assessment
- *detail* staffing provision for special needs ie

    Special educational needs co-ordinator (SENCO), non-teaching support assistants, parental helpers, specialist support services etc
- *include* Annual Reviews and Reports on SEN provision made to parents

All documentation should be adequate, relevant and up to date

Documentation: A Further Check List

Documentation, general and specific, will be required on the following:
- The aims and objectives of the school
- School prospectus and other information packs
- School development plan
- Timetabling arrangements
- Staff responsibilities
- Minutes of governing body meetings and annual reports
- Financial details. including all sources of funding
- Links with other schools and outside bodies
- Details of any particular initiatives or projects

SEN Implementation

Prior to the inspection the inspectors will have analysed the documentation and information and identified the issues they will need to investigate which will include:

- delivery of the National Curriculum
- implementation of the Code of Practice
- integration of special educational needs into the School Development Plan
- full and sensitive record keeping systems
- potential integration and re-integration programmes
- links between therapy and teaching
- links between residential and other schools
- links with parents
- links with carers and support services
- equality issues relating to ethnicity and gender
- staff training and development

> **Evidence should exist of a common policy for identifying children with special educational needs and for providing a broad and balanced curriculum for all**

SEN Policy and Practice: Key Questions

Key questions for an inspection team are likely to be:

- What strategies are in operation for helping identified children eg statemented pupils, those with specific problems, the able and talented etc?
- Are those strategies effective?
- How much do pupils' standards improve from entry to exit?
- Is there a record system which details the effectiveness of the strategies deployed?
- Is this information available to all concerned including parents?
- Is there a policy of involving parents which is regularly reviewed?
- How involved are support services, educational psychologists and other agencies?
- How aware are the governors with responsibilities for special educational needs of policy and practice within the school?
- What priority is given to special educational needs by senior management, middle management and governors?

The inspection team will want to probe a schools' commitment to special educational needs, to check that policies are translated into practice, and that pupils and parents are satisfied with the educational and pastoral care they are given.

Statements and Annual Reviews

Statements and assessment

All schools must realise the statements of special educational needs and the last annual review are legal documents and are carefully scrutinised during the inspection process. These are an important part of the whole school assessment and recording systems.

How schools have regard to the Code of Practice at all stages will increasingly form a focus for inspection. Schools should be clear on their:
- assessment procedures
- recording of progress
- reports to parents/carers

Whenever possible the young person should be **fully** included and involved in the process.

Annual reviews

The importance of the annual review and the involvement of the young person and their parents/carers is paramount.

Plans should include agreed targets.

The annual review meeting should:
- review the progress made by the young person
- review the effectiveness of the last IEP and targets
- review the contribution made by the parents/carers
- include any updating of information
- agree and discuss future action

The inspection team will be very concerned that statements are being fully implemented, statemented young persons and their parents/carers are fully involved in decisions involving their well-being and that annual reviews are conducted properly and thoroughly

Extending the Experiences of SEN Pupils

Inspectors will want to know whether the school provides activities and uses the local community to extend the personal, social and direct experiences of pupils with special educational needs. These might include:

Activities

- sports
- drama
- music
- dance
- lunch-time clubs
- day trips
- field work opportunities
- travel

etc

Local community involvement

- leisure facilities
- community services
- local businesses
- voluntary activities
- inter school collaboration
- links with local colleges
- work experiences

etc.

The extended curricular activities are deemed to be a significant part of the experiences afforded pupils with special educational needs

SEN Focus During the Inspection

The areas that will be taken note of during the inspection include:
- Senior management support for special needs
- Relationships with other colleagues/subject areas
- Liaison with outside agencies and the community
- Awareness and sensitivity of staff
- Attitudes of pupils
- Quality of accommodation and resourcing
- Evidence of forward planning
- Strategies for dealing with statemented pupils

The effective classroom

The effective classroom will have evidence of:
- planning differentiated work
- targeting differing needs and abilities
- flexible learning strategies
- encouraging motivation and enhancing self-esteem
- promoting peer group collaboration
- consistency in monitoring and evaluating work

Lesson Observation

In preparing lessons to be observed during the inspection week it is important to immediately convey what is going on, numbers of pupils, what the task is, continuity and so on. There are a number of ways of achieving this:

- Make available a brief resumé based on an agreed school proforma to the inspector on entering the room. This should contain the lesson plan, links with the National Curriculum. etc

- Arrange for a pupil to explain the lesson, the work being undertaken and how it relates to previous work providing this does not interrupt the lesson

- Provide a pen portrait, preferably with a photograph, of pupils with extra special needs

- Provide the inspector with:
  - a sample of an individual's work over an extended period
  - some assessment of progress/achievement made

- Provide, where possible any video or photographic evidence in advance

---

Time is extremely limited and it is appreciated if you provide the inspector not only with lesson details but the full context within which the lesson is taking place.

Special Units in Mainstream Schools

Specialist teams will inspect SEN Centres/Units for statemented pupils eg:
- specific learning difficulties
- hearing/visually/speech impaired
- emotional/behavioural difficulties

The school should negotiate with OFSTED for the concurrent inspection of any on- or off-site centre as part of the normal inspection. It is important that this is detailed in the initial inspection forms that the school completes.

The centre is subject to the same process as stated in the *Framework for the Inspection of Schools*.

The main focus of the inspection will be the Individual Educational Plans (IEPs) that are applied by the teaching and support staff in respect of each pupil.

The documentation and optional information provided by the centre will be analysed by the team and issues for inspection identified in advance.

The inspection will also focus on:

- organisation and management
- statements
- annual reviews
- liaison with parents
- links with other mainstream and special schools
- contacts with external specialists

etc

Special centres/units are subject to the same stringent inspection procedures as mainstream schools and are inspected as part of the whole school inspection

Special Schools

Special schools are subject to the same inspection procedures as mainstream schools although there is specific guidance to inspectors which schools should carefully study. They need to be very clear about:

1. How the specific needs of pupils are met
2. What their policy is with regard to pupils with additional needs
3. How particular gifts/talents of pupils are encouraged
4. How the National Curriculum is being delivered
5. How they deliver subjects and the time allocated to them at each Key Stage
6. How extra support and help is deployed
7. How specialist aids or equipment are used
8. What additional specialist professional development is available
9. How closely parents/carers are involved
10. How the school uses statements and annual reviews to inform planning
11. How carefully the progress of pupils is monitored
12. How well progress is reported to parents/carers
13. How additional support eg counselling/therapies is given
14. How effective the links between teachers/support staff, therapists and other professionals
15. How teachers/support staff link with care staff in a residential setting
16. How much involvement there is with other schools/colleges
17. How links with the community/local business are cemented
18. How transition routes to the next stage of education/life are managed

> **Special schools must be clear about their role and their aims. They must be specific about what they offer and how effective they are in using a range of support to enhance the quality of life for their pupils.**

SEN and the School Development Plan

School development plans usually span 3–5 years and detail areas for development, responsibilities, target dates, how their success/implementation is to be monitored and evaluated and possible costs. Broad areas might be:

Curriculum
- development of the National Curriculum
- differentiation strategies to be implemented
- cross curricular themes
- balancing timetable provision

Resources
- development of resources
- development of physical resources
- resource improvements
- financial priorities

Staffing
- deployment of responsibilities
- developing role of the SENCO
- developing role of non-teaching staff
- staff development

Teaching and Learning
- team building
- classroom observations
- teaching and learning styles
- raising standards

Management
- aims, vision and direction
- policy development
- consultation processes
- lines of communication
- self review

Planning, assessment and recording
- developing IEPs
- review procedures
- records of achievement
- evaluating effectiveness

Pupils
- recruitment
- groupings
- pupil involvement and evaluation
- behaviour

External relationships
- parental involvement
- interaction with the community
- forming partnerships with other schools and colleges
- links with local businesses
- links with other agencies

While an inspection team will not expect every aspect of provision to be fully developed they, quite reasonably, will want to know what plans the school has for improving facilities, resources and delivery for special needs pupils. The school development plan should indicate this.

SEN: Further Evaluation Questions

Pupils
- Do all pupils have access to all subjects regardless of their ability?
- Are pupils fully aware of their IEPs and individual targets?
- Are pupils actively involved in planning, recording and evaluating their own learning programmes wherever feasible?
- Are pupils given regular and relevant feedback on their progress?

Management
- Does the school promote a climate of warmth and support?
- Is there sensitivity to individual needs?
- Are pupils encouraged to take risks without fear of criticism?

Administration
- Is the Register up to date and comprehensive?
- How effective are the recording and monitoring arrangements?
- Are the IEPs in place and working?

Teaching
- Are tasks matched to pupils' needs?
- Is there a variety of teaching models deployed?
- Is account taken of pupils' differing learning styles?
- Are pupil groupings flexible to allow for maximum interaction?
- Is co-operative learning encouraged?
- What opportunities are there for direct experience?
- Are study skills promoted?
- Are flexible learning strategies used?

Resources
- Are pupils with SEN adequately resourced?
- Is there easy access to resources?
- How effectively is Information Technology used?

Working areas
- Does the layout and appearance of the working areas promote learning?
- Are resource bases properly resourced and used?
- Is pupils' work displayed to good effect?

Support
- Where available are support staff used effectively?
- How available is specialist advice through the schools psychological service, support teams etc?
- Is there an effective parent partnership arrangement?
- What opportunities are there for professional development?

Communication
- How well do staff interact and communicate?
- How involved are governors?
- Is there communication and involvement with other schools and institutions?
- How extensive are the school's efforts to communicate with and involve parents/carers?

The Special Educational Needs Co-ordinator (SENCO)

According to the Code of Practice the responsibilities of the teacher designated as the co-ordinator in mainstream schools are:

- the day-to-day operation of the school's SEN policy
- liaising with and advising fellow teachers
- co-ordinating provision for children with special educational needs
- maintaining the school's SEN register and overseeing the records on all pupils with special educational needs
- liaising with parents of children with special educational needs
- contributing to the in-service training of staff
- liaising with external agencies including the educational psychology service and other support agencies, medical and social services and voluntary bodies

Department for Education (1994) Code of Practice on the Identification and Assessment of Special Educational Needs, DfE 9–10

In small schools this role may be part of the headteacher or deputy headteacher's role. In larger schools there may be a SENCO and a supporting team.

> **The Governing Body should look carefully at the timetable of such staff to ascertain if there are any constraints on them in fulfilling the school's legal responsibilities and delivering the recommendations of the Code of Practice.**

The Dynamic Role of the SENCO

The specific responsibilities of a SENCO, according to the Code of Practice, does not necessarily describe the role they are performing in the school. SENCOs may wish to take note of an attempt made to clarify the *dynamic* role they often occupy within an institution.

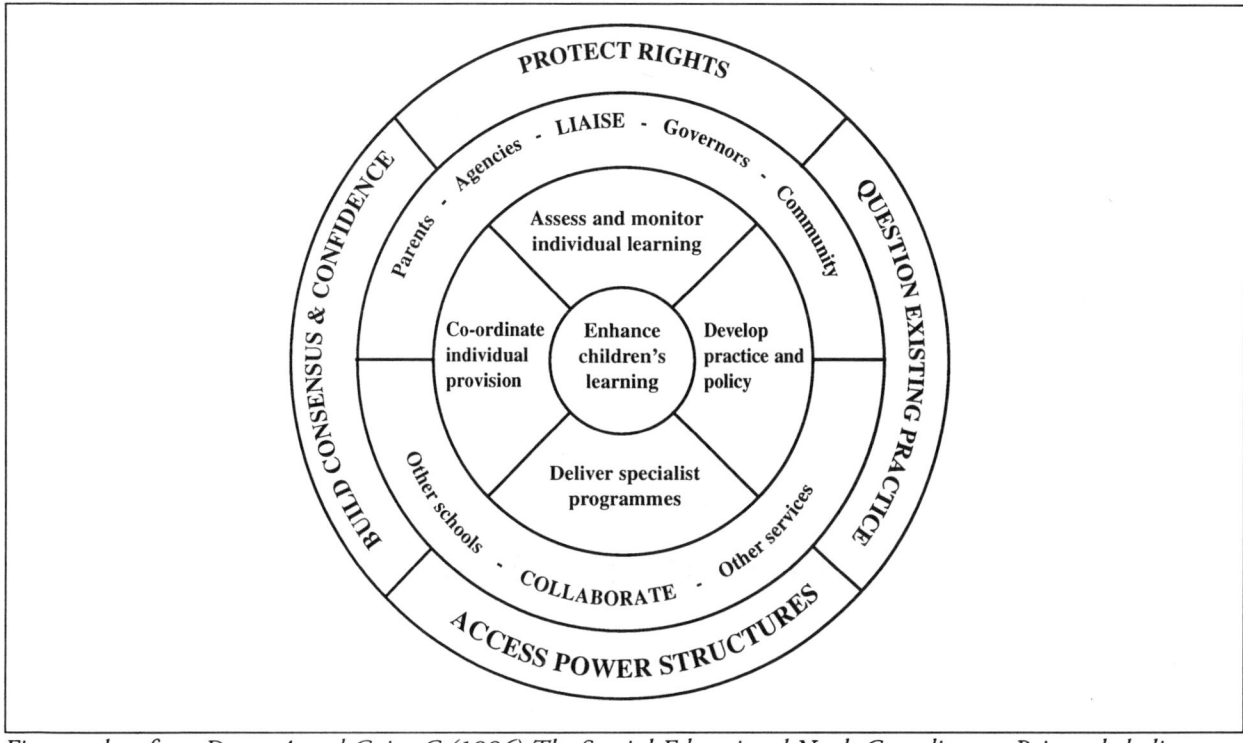

Figure taken from Dyson A and Gains C (1996) The Special Educational Needs Co-ordinator: Poisoned chalice or crock of gold? in Gains, Charles (1996) The Special Educational Needs Co-ordinator, NASEN Tamworth.

- The core *purpose* of enhancing children's learning which remains central to SENCO's responsibilities.
- The *co-ordination role* which involves bringing together assessment and monitoring procedures, the development of policy and practice, co-operating with colleagues and the oversight of specialist strategies and programmes.
- Increasingly there is a *liaison and collaborative function* that looks to consult and involve others beyond the immediate confines of school.
- Finally there is an *implicit role*, rarely stated, that sees the SENCO acting as advocate, consensus builder, even power broker.

> **The role of the SENCO is much broader and more complex than the description given in the Code of Practice. SENCOs should examine this and bring to the attention of an inspection team those aspects of their role that stretch beyond the confines of that simple description.**

Post Inspection

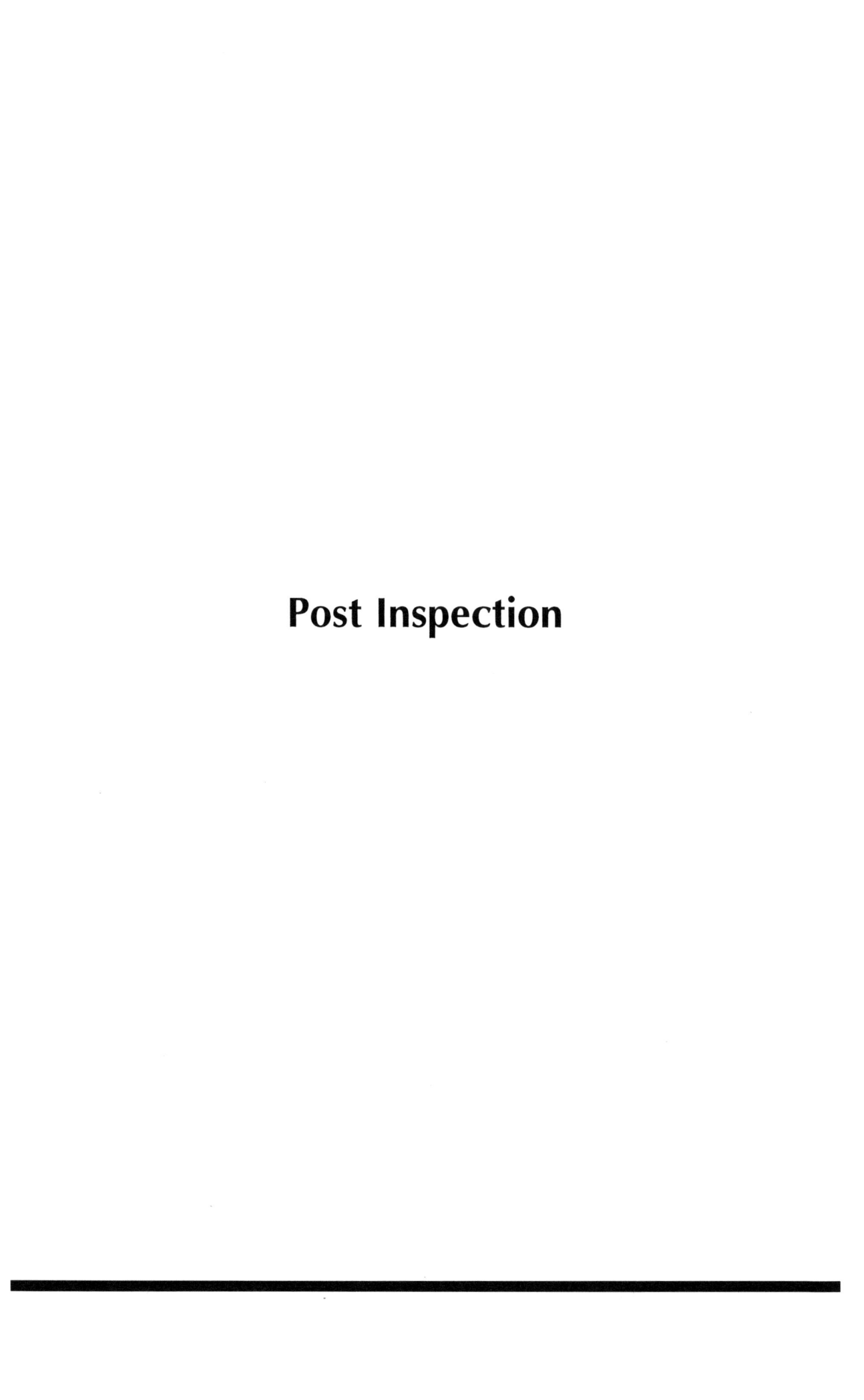

Interviewing Co-ordinators

Inspectors interviewing co-ordinators might pose some questions to ascertain their influence on:

Quality of teaching

Is this achieved by:
- working alongside colleagues?
- staff development programmes?
- information provision?
- discussion of particular problems or pupils?
- building resources?
- organising additional help?

Quality of learning

Is this achieved by:
- planning programmes/lessons?
- facilitating differentiation?
- improving teaching methods?
- enhancing self image?

Standards of achievement

Is this facilitated by:
- assessment, record keeping and reviews?
- records of achievement?
- a range of accreditation?
- close working with and mentoring of pupils?
- regular communication with parent/carers?
- systematic self review processes?

Inspectors will be wanting to know the effectiveness or otherwise of those staff with responsibilities for special educational needs.

The Report

At the end of the Inspection the Registered Inspector will make a verbal report to the headteacher and/or senior management team and later to the governors on the team's findings and judgements which allows for any factual inaccuracies to be corrected.

- The written report will be presented within 5 weeks of the end of the inspection.
- The report will follow the pattern laid down in the Framework using the same section headings
- The main findings of the report, along with key points for development, will be at the beginning of the report
- A summary of the report must be made available to parents by the school (see Appendix C)
- A copy of the report and the summary must also be submitted to Her Majesty's Chief Inspector

Special educational needs

Special educational needs will be included in all the main areas of the report and there will be:

- A statement about standards of achievement made by SEN pupils
- Comments on the effectiveness of SEN policies, arrangements and organisation including statutory requirements
- Identification of any key issues or actions that need to be addressed in relation to pupils with special educational needs

---

The Inspection Report is made to the Governing Body and they are responsible for formulating and implementing the Action Plan which follows an inspection

The Action Plan

Following an inspection every school must produce an Action Plan. The law normally places the responsibility for this on the Governing Body. The Action Plan must be prepared within 40 working days of receipt of the report from the Registered Inspector. It should set out the steps the Governing Body intend to take to tackle the issues raised in the report.

For each key issue the Action Plan should:
- quote the issue from the report and outline the tasks needed to tackle it
- state clearly and in detail what action will be taken
- ensure the proposals can be achieved and monitored
- set deadlines for action either short term (3 months), medium term (18 months) or long term (over 18 months)
- state the resources needed whether this requires the use of existing resources more effectively or acquiring new resources
- name the person(s) responsible for ensuring the required action is taken
- identify who will be asked to help with the action either from within or outside the school
- state how progress in tackling the issues will be monitored, who has responsibility for this, and to whom they will report

In preparing an Action Plan it is helpful to see whether it is necessary to revise the School Development Plan in the light of the report and when!

After completing the Action Plan the Governing Body must send it within five days to:
- the parents of all pupils registered at the school
- everyone who is employed at the school
- OFSTED
- the local education authority (for an LEA school) or the Secretary of State (for a self governing school)
- those who appoint the foundation governors (where applicable)
- the local Training an Enterprise Council (for a secondary school)

> **Copies must also be made available to any member of the public and a single copy free to anyone living within three miles of the school upon request. Progress made in implementing the Action Plan should be detailed and reported in the annual report to parents. Questions may also be asked about it at the annual parents meeting.**

After the Inspection

There will be an inevitable 'hangover' as the tension subsides but Senior Management should:

- make careful arrangements for feedback sessions with staff
- consider whether the Summary is all that should be sent to parents. Some schools have included their own observations and held special meetings to explain this to parents
- prepare to deal with the media... produce a press release
- link the Action Plan with the School Development Plan
- use the inspection process in a positive way to develop provision, improve standards and relationships with those involved in the school

---

Inspection should be seen as part of a constructive, self reviewing and improving process and part of an on-going developmental process

References

Core References (Office for Standards in Education)

Framework for the Inspection of Schools – October 1995*

The OFSTED Handbook – Guidance on the Inspection of Secondary Schools October 1995, HMSO

The OFSTED Handbook – Guidance on the Inspection of Nursery and Primary Schools – October 1995, HMSO

The OFSTED Handbook – Guidance on the Inspection of Special Schools – October 1995, HMSO

The OFSTED Handbook – Inspection Resource Pack – October 1995, HMSO

Relevant References (Office for Standards in Education)

OFSTED Inspection: Answering Your Questions*

School Inspections – Understanding the New System*

School Action Plans: Planning for Improvement*

Understanding Action Plans*

Planning Improvement – Schools' Post Inspection Action Plans, HMSO Keeping your Balance*

*Free from OFSTED publications, PO Box 6927, London E3 3NZ

HMSO Orders: 0171 873 9090

National Association for Special Educational Needs (NASEN)

NASEN publish a number of relevant booklets:

Bill, Graham. Governor's Guide to Special Educational Needs in Mainstream Schools
Catalogue
No. HH1

Gains, Charles. The Special Educational Needs Co-ordinator

Catalogue No. NR1

Gordon, Mike and Smith, Hazel. Policy Development for Special Educational Needs: A Secondary School Approach
Catalogue No PD1

Luton, Kathleen. Policy Development for Special Educational Needs: A Primary School Approach Catalogue No. PD2

NASEN. Educational Entitlement: A Statement of Principles

Catalogue No. NG12

Warin, Stella. Implementing the Code of Practice: Individual Educational Programmes Catalogue No. IEP1

Address: NASEN House, 4/5 Amber Village, Amber Close, Amington, Tamworth, Staffs B77 4RP

Other references

Advisory Centre for Education (ACE) (1995) Special Education Handbook. London

Audit Commission/HMI (1992) Getting in on the Act: A Management Handbook for Schools and LEAs. London: HMSO

Audit Commission/HMI (1992) Getting the Act Together: Provision for Pupils with Special Educational Needs. London: HMSO

Byers, Richard. Planning the Curriculum for Pupils with Special Educational Needs David Fulton: London

Department for Education (DfE) (1994) The Code of Practice on the Identification and Assessment of Special Educational Needs. DFE and the Welsh Office

Landy, Maria (1994) Preparation for School Inspection, *Support for Learning*, 9 (1)

Ramjhun Ahmed F. (1995) Implementing the Code of Practice for Children with Special Educational Needs: A Practical Guide. David Fulton: London

Rose, Richard, Ferguson, Ann, Coles, Caroline, Byers, Richard and Banes, David (1996) Implementing the Whole Curriculum for Pupils with Learning Difficulties. David Fulton: London

Appendices

Appendix A

Pupil Responses: Attainment, Attitudes and Progress

Attainment

What do the pupils know?
What do they understand?
What can they do?
How does it compare with national standards?
Are all pupils challenged and achieving well?

Attitudes

Are pupils involved?
Are they enjoying the lesson?
Are they proud of their work?
Are they working independently?
Are they working collaboratively?
Can they take responsibility?
Can they concentrate and stay on task?
Are relationships with one and other positive?
Do they show respect for other's feelings?
Do they show respect for other's work?
Do they relate well with staff?

Progress

Are the pupils gaining in knowledge and understanding?
What skills are they acquiring or developing?
Are they building on prior learning?
How does this activity relate to further learning and development?
Do they know how to research a topic?
Do they have problem solving skills?
Can they pose the right sort of questions?
Can they share and convey ideas?

Observing pupil attainment, attitudes and progress is the main priority of inspection

Appendix B
Quality of Teaching: Key Points

Does the teacher:

- plan well?
- have a secure knowledge of what is being taught?
- set high expectations?
- use effective methods and approaches to meet the needs of all pupils?
- control the class effectively?
- promote good attitudes and behaviour?
- check pupils' work regularly?
- provide feedback to pupils?
- demonstrate signs of personal development?

Teaching is graded as follows:

Grade 1 Excellent
Grade 2 Very good – promotes high standards
Grade 3 Good
Grade 4 Satisfactory – promotes sound standards
Grade 5 Unsatisfactory
Grade 6 Poor – promotes very low standards
Grade 7 Very poor

Appendix C

Summary of the Inspection Report

This takes the following format:

THE SCHOOL

A brief description of the school indicating such factors as its:
- nature
- phase
- number of pupils
- number of staff

INSPECTION FINDINGS

This selects from the Report and reiterates the main findings and key points for the school to act on:
- *Standards.* Judgements regarding all subjects inspected at each Key Stage
- *The Quality of Education.* Judgements related to the teaching of pupils and their responses
- *Efficiency.* Judgements regarding value for money, management and leadership
- *Spiritual, moral, social and cultural developments.* Judgements about each of these aspects

WHAT THE SCHOOL SHOULD DO NOW

The Inspection team will draw attention to those elements they consider should be maintained or improved eg
- maintain the present ethos and preserve the successful spiritual, moral, social and cultural development of the pupils
- review the school development plan giving more precise details and costings
- develop schemes of work to support classroom practice and ensure progression and continuity is achieved throughout the school
- implement further the Code of Practice
- identify more effectively staff needs in relation to special educational needs
- improve the use of information technology across the curriculum

etc